I'm Thinking of a Backyard Animal

Bela Davis

Abdo Kids Junior
is an Imprint of Abdo Kids
abdobooks.com

Abdo Kids
I'M THINKING OF AN ANIMAL

abdobooks.com

Published by Abdo Kids, a division of ABDO, P.O. Box 398166, Minneapolis, Minnesota 55439.

Printed in the United States of America, North Mankato, Minnesota.

052024

092024

THIS BOOK CONTAINS RECYCLED MATERIALS

Photo Credits: Getty Images, Shutterstock, ©Sadie the dog p.23

Production Contributors: Teddy Borth, Jennie Forsberg, Grace Hansen

Design Contributors: Candice Keimig, Pakou Moua

Library of Congress Control Number: 2023948535

Publisher's Cataloging-in-Publication Data

Names: Davis, Bela, author.

Title: I'm thinking of a backyard animal / by Bela Davis

Description: Minneapolis, Minnesota : Abdo Kids, 2025 | Series: I'm thinking of an animal | Includes online resources and index.

Identifiers: ISBN 9798384900528 (lib. bdg.) | ISBN 9798384901228 (ebook) | ISBN 9798384901570 (Read-to-me eBook)

Subjects: LCSH: City animals--Juvenile literature. | Questions and answers--Juvenile literature. | Riddles--Juvenile literature. | Animals--Juvenile literature. | Zoology--Juvenile literature.

Classification: DDC 591.756--dc23

Table of Contents

Guess the Animal!

I'm thinking of a backyard animal. Can you guess what it is?

I'm thinking of an animal that has a tail.

clues

- has a tail

But it is not a chipmunk!

I'm thinking of an animal that is a **mammal**.

clues

- has a tail
- mammal

But it is not a rabbit!

I'm thinking of an animal that has claws.

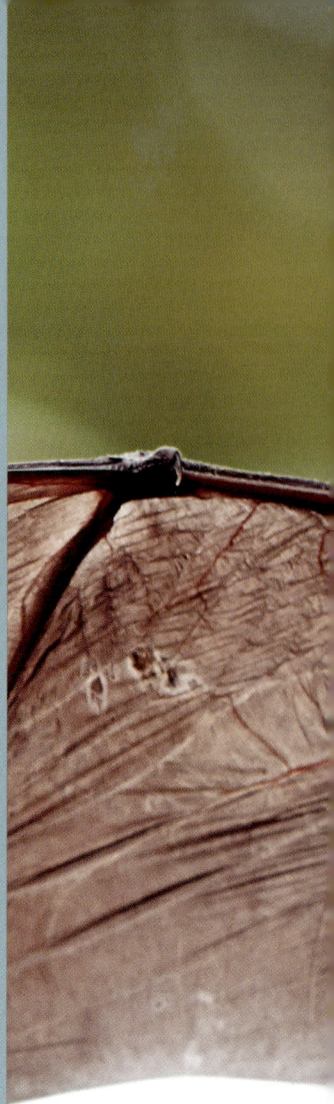

clues

- has a tail
- mammal
- has claws

But it is not a bat!

I'm thinking of an animal

that is gray.

clues

- has a tail
- mammal
- has claws
- gray

But it is not a squirrel!

I'm thinking of an animal that is **nocturnal**.

clues

- has a tail
- mammal
- has claws
- gray
- nocturnal

But it is not a rat!

I'm thinking of an animal that has rounded ears.

clues

- has a tail
- mammal
- has claws
- gray
- nocturnal
- has rounded ears

But it is not an opossum!

Do you know what animal I'm thinking of?

clues

- has a tail
- mammal
- has claws
- gray
- nocturnal
- has rounded ears

I'm thinking of a raccoon! Now it's your turn! What animal are you thinking of?

Comparing Animals

	rabbit	bat	squirrel	raccoon
tail	✓	✓	✓	✓
claws	✓	✓	✓	✓
gray in color			✓	✓
nocturnal		✓		✓

Glossary

mammal
a warm-blooded animal with fur or hair on its skin and a skeleton inside its body.

nocturnal
active at night.

Index